Accompanied

Poetry by
"Twinkle" Marie Manning

Matrika Press

Accompanied
Copyright © Marie Manning
Originally published February 2021
Republished November 2025

All Rights Reserved
including the right of reproduction,
copying, or storage in any form
or means, including electronic,
In Whole or Part,
without prior written permission of the author.

ISBN: 978-1-946088-55-0
Library of Congress Control Number: 2021931876

1.Poetry 2.Spirituality 3.Philosophy 4.Title

Cover Image: Resin art by Joscelyne Drew, Surf & Earth Designs

Matrika Press

Matrika Press
www.MatrikaPress.com
www.TwinklesPlace.org

#LivingLifeAsAPrayer

For my children and grandchildren.

Contents

8. Listen
9. Emergent Green
10. Deep in the Forest
11. The Forest, It Lay Bare Now
12. Be Like the Trees
13. Trees a brighter color-guard
14. June's Calling
16. Colors of June
18. Nature's Last Gold
19. Morning Dove
20. Morning by the River
21. The Reconciliation of Oneness
23. He Beckoned Me Forward
25. She shelters me in the grace of a silent moon
26. Bench. Beauty. Beholder.
27. Councils, Revisited
29. Holy Love
30. Pray. Wait. Trust.
31. Peace is the Way
32. Om Tara Tu Tara
33. Beauty Appearing

35. Beauty is Born
37. A Time for Everything
38. Last Star I See Tonight
42. To the Sacred Inside
44. The Calling
46. Simplicity you grant such sweet solace
47. Do You Pray?
48. My Breath Set to Her Rhythm
50. Circling but Never Reaching Silence
51. A Parable
52. Undoubted Love
53. Fog
54. Pillars in the Menagerie of Attributes
58. Shower Tears
59. Not to be Extinguished
61. My Beloved Self
63. My Cailleach Autumn Song
64. Howling Winds Shall Cease
66. Sample Utility
67. Centrifugal Forces Renounced
68. When Goodbye Looks Like an Ordinary Day
70. My Night's Flight
71. a horror poem
73. When a Heart Breaks Open in the Forest

74. For the Grief Stricken
75. The Triage of Grief
76. Grief Brings Friends
77. Beauty
78. Looking Life in the Eye
80. The Dark Season
81. They ask if I want to see your body
82. You Changed Everything
83. The Afterward
85. She Stood There

Listen

Breathe in each morning the magick of Life. Breathe out each evening deep gratitude for living. And Listen to the Call of the Universe
in every interaction,
in every curve in the road,
in every commitment to task,
in every covenant of relationship,
in every whispered word,
in every meditation,
in every prayer,
in every song;
Listen.

Emergent Green

Green like no other;
spectrums full,
lengths of trees adorned in
pigments persuaded by daylight,
tilt toward yellow.

Spring has arrived;
Summer soon to follow;
Life in Maine as it should be.

What questions must we ask
to realize our purpose?
Can we know the unknown?
Can we seek the unsearchable?

Green like no other;
spectrums full,
lengths of trees adorned in
pigments persuaded by daylight,
tilt toward yellow.

Could that we would
understand what's before us;
unspeakable majesty awaits
the awakening soul.

Deep in the Forest

Deep in the forest,
Quiet shapes the sound of immense emollient twilight.
Saturated shades of perpetual green caress the sky.
Blues sink down to violet.
Leaves land lightly;
    Layering lanes to linger upon.
Seekers of silence satisfied,
Within this modulating animated tenement.
Sanctuary of Solace found beneath copious canopies of trees;
Living, Breathing.

The Forest, It Lay Bare Now

The forest, it lay bare now.
Trees no longer
Reach the sky;
The bird no place to land.
Trees no longer
Transform the air;
The bird no place to land.
Ask thou please,
Transform the air;
Impossible the plight.
Ask thou please,
Replant the trees;
Impossible the plight.
We need our roots;
Replant the trees.
The children cry,
We need our roots.
Reach the sky,
The children cry;
The forest, it lay bare now.

a pantoum poem

Be Like the Trees

May you stand tall 'til the end of your days.
Deep roots.
Inner strength.
Radiant exterior.
Stretching high.
Flexible where you stand.
Letting go when it's time.
Offering comfort and beauty to all
who are so fortunate to be in your presence.

Trees a brighter color-guard

Springtime I hear you calling.
Just around the corner,
Your arrival is upon us.
As rain washes Winter away,
Just around the corner.
From two more blustery storms,
As rain washes Winter away,
And we pick up the fallen branches
From two more blustery storms.
Grass begins to grow,
And we pick up the fallen branches,
Flowers and blossoms emerge;
Grass begins to grow.
Birds make return flights home,
Flowers and blossoms emerge;
Trees a brighter color-guard,
Birds make return flights home.
Your arrival is upon us.
Trees a brighter color-guard;
Springtime I hear you calling.

a Springtime pantoum

June's Calling

May your approach
be as a whisper,
caress my cheek
so I know you're there.

Tap my window
with melodic raindrops,
send gentle winds
to mess my hair.

Plant yourself
along the roadside,
appear in daffodils
spirited display.

Fill the air with
puffs of dandelions,
help me remember
how we'd play.

Send the bees
to nurse the lilacs,
that their scents
warm my heart.

Manifest
in gentle sounds,
each day inly
works of art.

Return each breath
once given,
surround us in peace
that comfort brings.

Release the folds
encumbered,
by Time's
ever moving ring.

Tap my window
with melodic raindrops,
send gentle winds
to mess my hair.

May your approach
be as a whisper,
caress my cheek
so I know you're there.

Colors of June

Day by day,
you take my breath
away;

Unexpected surprise
morning brings
to my eyes.

'Yes,' I say,
as I awake each
day.

At your dawn
I ease out to
my lawn.

Blessedly alone,
I feel Earth's vibrations
being sown.

In gratitude and pleas
I sink to my
knees;

With dreams fulfilled,
present moment
without guilt.

Sitting surrendered in this grass,
allowing time to simply
pass.

So unlike
the public me,
who shines too tritely;

When what I desire
most is stillness
unmired.

Carefree silence belongs
alongside
Chickadees' songs;

Colors of June
no mere ornaments
when in bloom.

Here,
when I'm
near,

Worship embarks;
my resonant
soul sparks.

Nature's Last Gold

If the first green is gold,
then the last gold
is green.

Such is life here
in Maine.

Morning Dove

The morning dove woke me and I knew
My truth at last.

Speaking it softly first,
Then with more strength,
Adjusting myself as I sat up;
Standing on the floor.
Going to the window,
Seeing her take flight,
I knew I was about to too.

Free at last,
My voice ready,
My life path clear again.

P.S.:
Yes, I know it is "Mourning" Dove...But she woke me each morning in Santa Barbara! So she became my Morning Dove especially since I was not in mourning.

Morning by the River

Charmed by the beauty of this River.

Breathing in the gentle breeze,
Listening to the rush of the water,
Watching rocks glisten,
Seeing the Sun rise beyond the tree line.

I place my heart and my hopes beside her bank.

Trusting this Exemplifier of Life,

And allowing
the Center of my truth
to Flow through
my already Awakened Purpose.

Gratitude fills me;
Spirit moves me;
My soul rejoices;

Morning has arrived once again.

The Reconciliation of Oneness

On days like this,
I walk.
Smiling, I tilt my face toward the sky;
fluffy white clouds
scattered thru blue heavens,
soft breezes breaking silence,
leaves moving gently,
trees standing still,
water lapping idly
at the riverbank's shore.

Sebasticook, like Life itself, moving onward.
I release a handful of dried flowers
thoughtfully into the shallows,
once alive in my garden across the road,
now to merge into the afterlife
where the Summerland awaits
the reconciliation of Oneness.

Season's successive revolutions are
the reconciliation of Oneness,
where Summerland awaits
now to merge into the afterlife.

Once alive in my garden across the road,
thoughtfully into the shallows
I release a handful of dried flowers.

Sebasticook, like Life itself, moving onward
at the riverbank's shore.

Water lapping idly,
trees standing still,
leaves moving gently,
soft breezes breaking silence,
scattered thru blue heavens.

Fluffy white clouds
smiling, I tilt my face toward the sky.

I walk,
On days like this.

He Beckoned Me Forward

The Chickadee's singsong
greeting me at the entrance,
"hel lo"
"hel lo"
He called to me;
beckoning me forward
into his sanctuary.

"Hello," I replied,
as I made my way down
the overgrown but discernible
path toward the pond
I had been told was there;
I had been told was beautiful;
I had been told would be quiet;
And they were right.

At first I wondered if the
two who gave directions
would follow;
they did not.
Then, I wondered if others
would be in the woods
seeking solace;
no one else was.

The woods were mine
and mine alone,
save for the Chickadee,
his song,
and the spirits who watch
over the land.

Sun-blessed trees.
Wind-cooled waters.
Deep roots saturated
in sacred soil.

Hours spent in silence.
Felt like days spent in contemplation.
Peace found on Earth;
one moment at a time;
each containing every.

Beyond his sanctuary,
beckoning me forward,
He called to me,
"hel lo"
"hel lo"
greeting me at the entrance;
The Chickadee's singsong.

She shelters me in the grace of a silent moon

She shelters me in the grace of a silent moon:
Rising,
Rising,
Almost unnoticed in the breadth of the sky.

Her new moon rises,
Fresh in an Evening's dawn;
Open to all that may enter,
Who seek divine guidance.

Searchers welcoming dark solitude,
Seeing brilliance beyond the shadow;
Moving,
Quietly.

Patiently ushering Knowing forth,
Building endurance under the heavenly cloak,
Wrapping All in invisible rays of light,
She shelters me in the grace of a silent moon.

Bench. Beauty. Beholder.

I love this bench.

It is worn and chipped away by the elements
and by use (and abuse).

It has witnessed both
pristine calm
and the ravages of storms.

Yet it sits here.

Sturdy and strong.

Embodying the beauty
in this beautiful location.

Beauty.

Beholder.

May I take heart in the strength of this bench. In the strength of benches like her. May I ever choose to Stay in dignity, instead of crumbling into the Void of denial.

Bench on Neptune Ave, La Jolla, CA

Councils, Revisited

She says, *"we must sit down and reason together."*
Close to the earth;
no platform, no stage.
In Circle;
Facing each other.
In small groups.
Easily able to to see and to hear who is speaking.
Without judgement, as if in the dark,
where the words matter most, not who is saying them.
Equal. We begin
to begin to listen.
Speaking softly. Saying our truths.
Affirming the Holy in each other and beyond us as we do.

"It is not I who speaks but the wind.
Wind blows through me.
Long after me, is the wind."

Long after us are the decisions we make in Councils.
When we truly value each other, we talk with each other.
Not at, or to, but with.
Our words honor each other.
Our words reflect the legacy we wish to leave for those who come next.
Our words are strong, yet gentle.
In this place we create together we are intentionally and mutually peaceable.

From this sacred space of mutual peaceableness we can express what is truly on our hearts and minds, without pretense, without pressure to conform this way or that way.
We can be brave knowing we are safe.
We can be flexible knowing no one here wants to break us.
We can trust we are all equal.
We can create the highest good for all.
And, we listen and act with love.

A response to "Councils" by Marge Piercy
from "Circles on the Water."

Holy Love

Make me an instrument of Love.
Deepen my ability to give
and to receive
precious gifts of the Spirit
made manifest by encounters
of Love.

Love without fears,
Love without walls,
Love with full connection.
Love that is free to blossom and grow.

Make me an instrument of Love
as I nurture sacred pastures
in the present
and eternal landscapes of Life.

One can experience love through one's default settings.
Or,
One can choose to mindfully experience love through
co-created, mutually-honoring, practices of love.

How can you tell the difference?
Quite simply:
How you feel.

How you feel is the indicator of and signal for what the
basis of your experience is.

Pray. Wait. Trust.

Pray.
Wait.
Trust.

Pray for peace to find its way into your heart, into the world.
Wait with perseverance as your companion in the dark still moments.
Trust that Love shall spread its wings in flight toward the spoken and unspoken desires of the heart, even as it accompanies peace unto thy shoulders and surrounds the world in its beloved embrace.

Pray.
Wait.
Trust.

Peace is the Way

Sing for peace. Dance for peace. Stand for peace.
Sit for peace. Talk for peace. Listen for peace.
Pray for peace. Act for peace.
Come together for peace.
Be Peace.

Because….
Peace is the Way.

#PulpitOfPeace

Om Tara Tu Tara

Think of a form of liberation you would like to bring into your reality.
Do you name it out loud, or hold it in silence?
There is more power in words spoken aloud.
Fear shrouds the silent wish;
Suffocating it in darkening silence.
The voice, your Voice, gives it Power.
Give it Life with the Spirit of your Muse.
You will find it planted in the warm Earth of your Soul;
Whispering to you as the Heart's desire.
It needs Air to Breathe;
It craves the Fire of your Passion;
It grows with the Water of Dedication;
Let it Sing.
Om Tara Tu Tara
Om Tara Tu Tara
Om Tara Tu Tara
Om Tara Tu Tara

*Inspired by Tara, the Goddess of Liberation
and her "Om Tare Tuttare Ture Soha" meditation chant.*

Beauty Appearing

Have you ever caught a glimpse of something beautiful?
Just a glimpse.
So you turn toward it.

Upon looking, it is still beautiful
But you really do not know what it is.

You look closer.

Beauty yes, but something more:
Depth.

Wonder fills you.
The unknown interrupts your walk.
Your journey pauses;
A crossroad appears;
Hmmm….

This is where I am at right now.
Catching glimpses of my beautiful future.
Not really knowing with clarity what is about to unfold.
Standing at the crossroad.
One that only appeared when I decided to stop my until then course:
And wait.
And look with curiosity at the glint that caught my eye.
My attention has turned.
My heart beats a gentler beat now;

One that is in harmony with my mission;
One that soothes even as it enlivens;
One that is constant.

I know not what lies before me.
I know not even what it is I am gazing upon.
But it feels good.
It feels right.
And I know it is mine
To choose to follow.
If I mote it be.

Beauty is Born

We all have it.
Inside,
Like a treasure, we guard it.
Our talent, Our vision, Our love, Our beauty
It is our gift.
Our gift to give;
Our gift too often held in fear of the rejection of it
Too often clamped closed like the tight bud of a rose
Safe within the confines of its layers.

We feel the tug of Nature's desire.
Learned behavior behaves like instinct,
Shutting down and closing in our wish
For us to loosen the cage in which we store our treasure.
Keeping in check our intuitive Knowing
To set it free;
To share it.

Fear faces the tender heart,
Shrouding it in the shadows of our darkest memories.

Another moment arrives,
With the cresting Sun on the Eastern horizon.
Unpleasant grip misses a beat,
Altering the balance of Power;
Unlocking the bolt,
Releasing the leash,

Making the Darkness wince.

Beauty is Born.

Inspired by: Hafiz –
"How did the rose ever open its heart and give to this world all its beauty? It felt the encouragement of light against its being, otherwise, we will remain too frightened."
(1315-1390)

A Time for Everything

With eternity in our hearts,
everything is made beautiful in its time.

a time to heal;
a time to build;
a time to laugh;
a time to dance;
a time to gather;
a time to embrace;
a time to mend;
a time for peace;
a time to love.

Scattered stones need weep no more, for the seeds planted and watered with tears of mourning give way to the seasons of happiness and the heavens rejoice as it is time.

*Inspired by Peter Gabriel's "The Book of Love"
and Ecclesiastes 3 (NIV) and this moment in Time.*

Last Star I See Tonight

Standing at a crossroad,
she tucked a wayward
strand of soft silky hair
behind her porcelain ear,
as the Winds of Motion
whipped at her temple
and wound her skirts tight
around her body.

Knowing,
every intersection
contains every moment.

She waited for the signs.

Lips now ripe
from worrying her teeth over them,
still she stood
as if immobility would
delay the inevitable Choices
that would change
the cartography of the course
soon to be charted before her.

Knowing,
every intersection
contains every moment.

She waited for the signs.

For even if her eyes could see
the multitudes of gossamer threads
weaving Time in Motion
in all their ubiquitous majesty,
how could she delineate
that which would lead her
where she most wanted to be,
and, if she could track the right line,
would she be allowed to make the jump?

Knowing,
every intersection
contains every moment.

She waited for the signs.

She knew the rules,
few that they are at these junctions,
as one must choose not at random
nor with intentional oscillations imposed,
rather, in alignment with prior choices-
-the chooser's prior choices-
and the prior choices of others they are journeying with,
thus preserving consolidation
and conservation of energies,
maintaining structures of function;
allowing realities to substantiate Realty.

Knowing,
every intersection
contains every moment.

She waited for the signs.

It was capitulated to be possible even by homogenized cynics of holograms,
that coincidences light the way
for those seeking to create their own miracles,
for those wanting to merge their existence
with the timeline of their other selves,
and the place where dreams come true.

Knowing,
every intersection
contains every moment.

She waited for the signs.

Training her eyes
to locate he whose song played in her heart;
he whose soul called and answered to her soul,
assiduously discerning which where-
-yes, *which where-*
he chose her as she chose him;
with hearts open to love,
minds open to trust,
bodies fitting perfectly,
life unfolding in boundless bliss.

*Knowing,
every intersection
contains every moment.*

She waited for the signs.

Until the last star she saw that night
had him crossing to meet her where she stood and then
they were one.

To the Sacred Inside

Does the Sacred inside
whisper like a Summer's warm waiting breeze?

or

    does

        She

            pace

like a caged lioness;

            roaring,
        slamming,
    willing,

Herself to break free from silent wantings?

Oh Sacredness, hear my solemn invocation
for truth to be revealed,
for knowingness to flow forth
from my lips,
from my pen,
from all I am,
as a river filled with healing waters.

May the words I share
        be both blessing and lesson to others.

May my walk on this Earthly plane reflect

Your Divinity in me
>> ushering forward
>>> higher understandings
>>> of love, compassion, and grace.

May unity and peace follow in the wake
>> of my speaking,
>> of my writing,
>> and of my being.

May my Light
cast doubt away,
assuage the sharpest skeptics,
mitigate difficult passages,
mend broken spirits.

>> Ever and All Ways.

The Calling

The Calling feels stronger now,
Clearer now, here.
In the noise I thought it must be one;
Revealed in stillness to be many,
Shown to be mine.

Knowing is the coveted chest,
Acting is the treasure within;
The opening of takes courage.

The Calling searches for a crevice;
Pushes, pulls, prods to find
An outlet for Its source.

Its key hidden among charms on a bracelet.
Appears delicate, fragile;
Embodies strength when activated.
With light shining behind it,
Shadows come into form.
Occupying sands in time,
The echoes of a too long sleep wane.
Remorse has no place for it suffocates joy;
Rest's desire is in balance.

The Calling seeks a response.
An unwritten denouement yet to be imagined,
Remains a moment longer.
What good can come of a life underwater?
Not seeing nor hearing the messages above,
Dormancy is set aside to rise.

Awake with understanding,
My vigil is one of gentle grace.

I choose to Stay and answer The Calling.

Simplicity you grant such sweet solace.

Do You Pray?

I pray daily and throughout the day – my life is a life of prayer. My journey with prayer has been an ever evolving one. At present prayer to me is surrender and gratitude. The first, surrender, is in communion with, and experience of, the Holy. The second, deep gratitude for the Holy and the many gifts in my life. The outward appearance of such prayers can be formal or spontaneous: intentional moments of stillness and silence, visualization, or active with writing, creating art, chanting or singing or drawing down the moon, walking in the woods and along the river, speaking out loud my heart's desires or giving a blessing, it is the lullabies with my child each night….prayer is even found in doing the dishes at my kitchen sink, and dancing in my living room.

#LivingLifeAsAPrayer

My Breath Set to Her Rhythm

My morning eyes drifting across the breadth of Her
Smooth lines:
>Rough edges,
>>Alluring,
>>>Lulling.

My breath set to Her rhythm:

Slowly;

In,

Out,

Patiently;

In,

Out,

Deliberately;

In,

Out.

Ever consistent in Her ability to carve new passages
Around,
> Over,
>> Through.

She, the source of sometimes inevitable destruction,
Softening each obstacle that comes across Her Path.

Remembering at all times:

She is One
> and part of many Ones.

As are We.

- an Ode to the Ocean, and, now, to our ocean-like Lake.

Circling but Never Reaching Silence

Silence does not truly exist,
Nor does stillness.
Not really.
Quiet and whispers, yes;
But not silence and stillness.

I sit here seeking silence.
What stillness I demonstrate;
The wind tousles my hair,
The pulse of my blood rhythmic in my ears,
What stillness I demonstrate.
Breath in, breath out.
The pulse of my blood rhythmic in my ears;
My breathing harmonizing with my heartbeat.
Breath in, breath out.
Oh so still, yet ever in motion;
My breathing harmonizing with my heartbeat,
Circling but never reaching Silence.
Oh so still, yet ever in motion;
The room echoes my Stillness,
Circling but never reaching Silence.
The window left open,
The room echoes my Stillness;
The wind tousles my hair,
The window left open,
I sit here seeking silence.

(a pantoum)

A Parable

Traveler:
I've been away for a long time and am on my way home.

Sage:
Ahhh. 'Home.' I have discovered something about that mythical place.

Traveler:
What have you discovered?

Sage:
Most of its residents wear glasses with lenses shaped in the form of larva – they cannot easily see the butterfly you've become; only the caterpillar you once were…

Undoubted Love

A life of abiding love, deep peace, tangible happiness and absolute acceptance is not found in the oft sought-after fictional "unconditional love," but rather the deeper "undoubted love." The kind of love where friendship and gratitude, mutual values and loyalty are the cornerstones. To love and be loved, actively, daily, undoubtedly, is the seed, the roots, the stem, the bud, the blossom and the flower of true love.

Seek Not Unconditional Love,
                but, rather,
                              Undoubted Love.

Fog

Prologue:
The darkness saturates this sacred space,
Like a malevolent fog suffocating lost wanderers.

Entreaty:
Fog,
Would that you could create your own Brigadoon;
Yet this is no fanciful, carefree place of wonder.
Disperse your fibrous residue;
Roll away into the distant past;
Cease creating deceptive numbness;
Dissipate so we can see.
Release the blinding hold you have on all present;
Unclutter the path of false landmarks;
Leave this region unblemished;
Allow us to find our direction.

Pillars in the Menagerie of Attributes

a quiet loneliness
is settling in...

why?

once the eye of a storm passes
and the remainder gushes though,
in my experience
with literal storms as well as emotional ones,
those hidden things begin to emerge;

as with the silence that precedes a hurricane,
when animals and insects alike seek shelter
and remain in the protected places they've secured to
weather the storm,
our emotions, likewise, often scatter to the far off reaches
of our minds and bodies,
observing from afar as the torrents (of actions) rain down
and the painful winds (of words) rip through a once
peaceful place;

usually, when the wrath has ended its violent sweep
our emotions, like the animals peeking out in the Afterward of Mother Nature's gale, begin testing the air,
assessing destruction, cleaning up remnants, gathering
supplies anew,

activity renews
and life reassembles itself,
if not in the exact manner it had before the storm,
certainly in a way that is recognizable;

downed power lines are repaired or replaced,
yards are cleaned up,
homes are rebuilt;
hearts and psyches are too,
and the finishing touches soon follow,
assuring that what we do matters
and that picking up the pieces
is the right thing to do;

many, many times this has been my experience.

but not now,

could it be that my emotions are so far scattered, so
deeply buried, that the numbness that contained them
through the most heinous parts of the storm, have locked
them away beyond recovery?

for where is the commotion of the clean-up?
the tidings of a new and happy day?
the activity that
commences....
yes, silence comes too, but after the activity, and the
silence then is one of contented relaxation;

yet,

the silence that sits with me now
is not one of peace,
is not one of contentment,
it is not even a comfortable acceptance of what was,
and what is;

no.
it is a deep discomfort,
a feeling similar to a bite of food that is lodged in one's throat,
or an ill-at-ease heartburn,
or stirring in the belly that follows a too-acidic meal
you know will soon expel itself
through one exit
…or another;

how long will this last?
how soon can I resume course?
when will I be able to digest the experience
and translate it into a healing balm?

for that is what I do;
that is how I know to cope;
that is what allows me to continue to exist;

such is the alchemy I've perfected,
the transmutation of the awful incidents of life
into beautiful lessons learned;

once that conversion takes place,

I am at peace,
I am wiser,
I am gentler,
I am stronger,
I am able to fully access my joy;

where is my Joy?
where is my Benevolent Heart?

how is it that both are eluding me?

have they abdicated their posts?

if so,
I shall remain incoherent,
for they were the pillars in the menagerie
of my attributes.

Shower Tears

Seeking refuge in the dark;
Sadness filters through her trembling body,
The shower hides her tears.
Pilfered Home, Broken Trust;
Sadness filters through her trembling body.
Friendships broken, Loyalties divided;
Pilfered Home, Broken Trust,
Picking up the pieces;
Friendships broken, Loyalties divided.
Fear of what cruelty is next,
Picking up the pieces;
Protecting children from shattered truths,
Fear of what cruelty is next.
Knowing the patterns of crippled minds and severed souls;
Protecting children from shattered truths.
Washing away sorrow and fears;
Knowing the patterns of crippled minds and severed souls.
The shower hides her tears,
Washing away sorrow and fears;
Seeking refuge in the dark.

a pantoum poem after our home was vandalized

Not to be Extinguished

you close your eyes for a moment,
just a moment,
for the will of the world
has exhausted you;
and in that moment
you feel a seemingly benevolent caress at your cheek;
in curiosity you lift your gaze to the touch,
to realize the lull was intended to deceive;
the tornado forming within eyesight's range
catches more speed,
moment by moment,
whipping and whirling,
the once gentle wind, now a raging gust;
pushing you back even as you lean into safety,
then beckoned elsewhere, it turns toward another target.

you close your eyes for a moment,
just a moment,
for the will of the storm
has exhausted you;
and in that moment
silence enters;
you feel a seemingly benevolent caress at your heart,
in curiosity you lift your gaze to the touch,
to realize the lull was intended to deceive;
the storm has returned, and brought with it friends;

two, then three more,
emerging from the dust and debris of the prior thrashings,
the pushing, now pulling,
whipping and whirling,
until,
you cannot
    catch
        your
            breath,
and you cannot
    close
        your
            eyes;

for a moment, you think to risk it all by emptying your heart,
for that which is empty cannot be stolen
but then you remember:

You are a light to this world.

And you face the storm
and shine.

My Beloved Self

My Beloved Self,
Pour your sacred breath
in to the parts of your heart
that are hurting.

Actively allow
your own love
from your own source
to fill the spaces
void of happiness.

Melt away
the sorrow and fear
you find hidden
in the crevices,
carved by those
who did not honor
your love.

Give your cells
so much affection
and so much joy,
by sharing with yourself
that part of you
you readily give to others.

Beloved,
your breath is sacred;

Your laughter is infectious.
Your smile alone lifts up
an entire room.

Breathe in the peace
you provide to others!

You radiate abundant affection.
You give unconditional compassion.

You have unwavering faith
in the success
that can be had
when partners commit
to one another.

You strive always for justice.

You are honest
and loyal,
and steadfast,
and trustworthy.

You have integrity beyond measure.
You are kind and have clear vision.

My beloved self,
bestow these gifts upon yourself
and watch your dreams come true.

My Cailleach Autumn Song

Tantalizing whispers begin at dusk;
They disappear at dawn,
So commences my Cailleach Autumn Song.
Nighttime creatures walk the rail;
They disappear at dawn.
The day is filled with hushed delight;
Nighttime creatures walk the rail,
Effecting crispy sounds.
The day is filled with hushed delight;
Red horizons dot the trees,
Effecting crispy sounds.
Pink hues on the bushes,
Red horizons dot the trees;
Oh what splendor October brings.
Pink hues on the bushes,
While dead ones lift the veil.
Oh what splendor October brings,
So commences my Cailleach Autumn Song.
While dead ones lift the veil,
Tantalizing whispers begin at dusk.

a pantoum poem inspired by Dante Alighieri's "Autumn Song."
(1265-1321)

Howling Winds Shall Cease

Beneath the red sky,
The shadows they are clear;
Never fading, even when the stars appear.
With thunder on the mountain,
Echoing of broken heart filled streets;
It feels like we are moving,
But I know we are standing still.

The deepest black forest meets
The Holliday-esque sounds of "Bye and Bye."
Our laughing starry-eyes
Striking the shadow
Glimmering in the rising sun.
I guess,
It feels like we are moving,
But I know we are standing still.

These trees, they're not haunted
and do not frighten me.
Deep as the blue sea
a hard rain falls,
a bird sings, while another bird flies.
Even so,
It feels like we are moving.
But, I know we are standing still.

Strange unbelievable truths:
A man of constant sorrow you need not be.
That's as plain as it can be.
For everything is not broken;
Things can fall together just as easily as apart.
Yet…
It feels… like we are moving,
But… I know… we are standing still.

Rapidly fading a-Changing times,
And when the moon is bright,
This shooting star will slip away forever one night.
We can sit on top of the world,
Or we can say goodbye.
Because,
It feels like we are moving,
But I know we are standing still.

Postlude:
And the art of love planted
Will be harvested with another,
With kind speaking and no confusion now;
For the answers will have arrived
On the once howling wind.

Sample Utility

radically attenuated affectations
of elusive epiphanies
acquiescing to odious edifices

foible found
beneath didactic euphemisms

symbolic substitutions
resist infantile tutors
targeting zero-sum game

Centrifugal Forces Renounced

Disbursed among fraudulent memories,
fractal realities
place into perpetual motion
centrifugal forces
fueled by Fear's inertia.

Wastelands provide little comfort
in the wake of the Tempest.

Filaments of Time
shed light on makeshift lives.
Untold stories unfold towards Destiny's gate,
fleeing center gives way to vernacular beauty.
Unsustainable chaos resigns in the presence of Truth.

Love marks the Divine in holy sacrament.

When Goodbye Looks Like an Ordinary Day

Love flows out between our kisses, meets our hearts
and merges with us;
Unity expresses fully when goodbye looks like
an ordinary day.
Minds and bodies are as one, eyes and smiles look upon
End's beginning's just begun,
Baruch bashan.

The blessings already are
The blessings already are
The blessings already are
The blessings already are

Your hands upon my face alternate in tender passion,
cupping;
Holding, clasping, pressing when goodbye looks like an
ordinary day.
Directing us, memory serves beyond its motive, tugging
clothes off;
Layers noted, fire burns when goodbye looks like an
ordinary day.
Baruch bashan.

The blessings already are
The blessings already are
The blessings already are
The blessings already are

Sun shines in your room, reminds us the world's around us still.
Cradled in sanguine embrace,
Our Souls take note of earlier days;
Happiness presides our emotions;
It guides the way when goodbye looks like an ordinary day.
Baruch bashan.

The blessings already are
The blessings already are
The blessings already are
The blessings already are

Baruch bashan;
Baruch bashan;
Baruch bashan;
Baruch bashan;
Baruch bashan.

Acceptance of an inevitable relationship end
inspired by the ancient words "Baruch bashan" in a post by
San Diego Mastermind Sister, Angela Travers, which means:
"The blessings already are,"
and to the tune of "Across the Universe" by The Beatles.

My Night's Flight

As I soar through my dreams,
I am free to observe the eagerness of my flight.
For here in my dreams, I can easily
escape the inescapable.
I can rely on the untamed, for I can tame it.
I am sure to achieve, for I am strong.
In my dreams I control my life course,
and am unwavered by the challenges therein.
Truly I can fly into the depths of the sky,
As I sway on the currents of the air.
Beneath the surface of the water, I too can slice through
Without concern for the natural laws
that should prohibit it.
Have you perhaps felt the break of a cloud,
As you pass through one dream to another?
I can not express the feeling of lightheartedness,
as I lift like a butterfly toward the sun.
Or the victory I sense, when I flee from violence,
as I move through the atmosphere one last time.
I awake with regret that I no longer can fly
in the day as the night.
Anxious I am to close my eyes once again,
to leap in the breeze as I might.

a horror poem

Mystery surrounds the time
When Dawn broke at Midnight and
The Sun never set.

Shadows,
They say shadows,
Are where the
Dark Ones dwell.

Yet, they are wrong.

Light burning brightly,
So brightly,
Unobstructed by the comfort
Shade provides,
Scorches the living Soul.

'Tis in the sinews of
Seared Souls
The Dark Ones feed.

For truly I say unto you,
You are blinded by the light.

In the glorious hour
Of your illumination
Your Soul becomes tender.

Tender Souls embrace the Yoke.

Benevolent yoke? Nay.
Say I, a noose!

Brighter, brighter.
Tighter, tighter.

Eyes wide,
Smiles fixed;
Peace and revelries,
Irrelevant mix.

Shadows descend
Split moments before
Your Soul is eaten.

Hmmm…

Stories,
Ancient and new,
Revere the light.

Bringers of the Dawn,
Indeed.

Let
    there
        be
           Light.

When a Heart Breaks Open in the Forest

When a heart breaks open
in the forest,
and no one is there
to hear it shatter,
has it really broken?

For the Grief Stricken

Moving forward is necessary; "moving on" is impossible. Our loved-one's death was more than a moment; their life is more than a memory. Their existence is ever-present as they shape our lives even now.

The Triage of Grief

They sat with me for hours in this spot.
Sometimes talking.
Much of the time just being still,
gazing at Autumn's tranquil beauty
and listening to the sounds of the Lake.
For some this may look like healing.
I know with experienced certainty it is not.
Not yet.
This, this is the perpetual triage of raw grief.
Keep the body still.
Regulate the breath.
Quiet the mind.
Assess the wound.
Allow tears, laughter or lethargy to come.
Keep in check the anger.
When there is energy, do something useful, purposeful.
Ardently cradle the sorrow when it assails.
Repeat.

Written just a few weeks after my
22 year old son died in 2019.

Grief Brings Friends

Grief is everything and more, and nothing and different, than what most believe it is. Until one is holding their own grief -and being gripped by it- they cannot grasp the breadth of it, and even then it is always subjective.

I believe the single unchanging ever-truth of grief is that when it is present, it brings with it nefarious friends: fear, anxiety, self-doubt, regret, guilt among the legion of foes to peace in our heart. Mind, with its memory and hindsight prophecy, plays a role too as it lies in wait ready to pounce; weaponizing thoughts of what once was, and what will never be.

Unguided grief takes its toll a thousand fold and in as many painful ways.

Beauty

Beauty,
Beholding herself in the mirror,
Cannot always see what the rest of us so clearly can.

Her eyes trained by the hand of experience cruel,
Fails to see in the peripheral of life.

Wounded,
She sees only what she perceives before her;
And it is clouded.

Forgetting to wipe the misty fog off the mirror,
She turns away, still not knowing the beauty she is.

Yet Beauty she remains,
And will ever be held so in our memory's eye.

*For Nancy, for Lauren, and for all who fail to see how
beautiful they, and meaningful their lives, are.*

Looking Life in the Eye

The mirror in the hallway reflected the depth of her pain.
She stopped.
Looked closer at the stranger.
Questions ran rampant through her mind.

Who is this woman in the mirror?
Why the stain of tears on her cheeks?
What in her life, past or present, was wounding her heart?
How could she alter the image to one of joy?

She took a breath.
Then another.
Thinking.
Always thinking.

She acknowledged she was looking life in the eye.
The life that had led her to this moment.
It was her journey.
She chose every step.

Even when confronted with the unthinkable,
Where every turn was fraught with despair,
And each consequence was only a lesser evil;
She alone determined the direction forward.

As she would now, determine the direction.
For her road to hold joy, she has to choose joy.
Was she strong enough to release the comfortable
Cloak of sorrow?
Would she finally recognize herself if she did?

*Written as the title poem for
"Looking Life in the Eye: Poets of Central Florida,
Volume Three" published in 2015 by CHB Media
and Positively Florida.*

The Dark Season

We are at the threshold of the Seasons,
the doorway to the Year,
when the Veil is thin,
and time passes amorphously.

We turn inward as the Darkness beckons us.
We welcome the warmth of the fire,
contemplating the mysteries of the Unseen.

We honor the soft ache in our hearts
for those we have lost:
the people,
the dreams.

And we rest.
For rest we must, to heal.

This is the cycle of death and rebirth;
release and renewal.

We cherish this time
as the lessons it offers
penetrate our knowing.

May we breathe in wisdom
and breathe out patience.

May we find comfort in the warm embrace
of The Dark Season.

They ask if I want to see your body

They ask if I want to see your body;
It's time to say goodbye.
My mind takes me to yesterday,
Your embrace still fresh in my memory.
It's time to say goodbye.
Strong arms, passionate kisses,
Your embrace still fresh in my memory;
Warm body, muscles everywhere,
Strong arms, passionate kisses,
Smiles as sweet as honey;
Warm body, muscles everywhere,
You trace your fingers above my heart;
Smiles as sweet as honey,
You kiss my face;
You trace your fingers above my heart,
I kiss your heart and your sinewy belly;
You kiss my face;
My mind takes me to yesterday,
I kiss your heart and your sinewy belly;
They ask if I want to see your body.

*a pantoum-style poem in beloved memory of
Brandon Southward aka "South."*

You Changed Everything.

You, having existed, changed everything.
You, having died, changed everything.

The Afterward

The Afterward comes at so many times in so many ways.
I urge you to walk into the Afterward;
Yes, run.
Then stop.
Face it.
Experience the pain, the turmoil and grief.
Consume the uncertainty until you extinguish it.
Take every ounce of the Afterward that you can grasp.
Gather it up.
Not in a tight unrecognizable way
Rather, loosely – like picking wild flowers from a field.
Reap it.
Thresh it.
Then let it go.
You need to go into the Afterward.
It is necessary to stay there for a while.
Find your peace; seek it should it be unclear.
Open your hand for help;
Know that it is near.
Accept that there is more than the Afterward.
There is the Next.
There is Life.
Live your life now.
Accelerate it.
You are alive;
Feel it.

Stunned by loss,
Sudden as it is or may seem,
Issues arise.
Deal with the distress.
The Afterward is not meant to be permanent;
You, only you, can make it so.
Your life will go on with or without you.
Release the Afterward.
Set the example.

Live.

I wrote "The Afterward" just after my father died in December 1999 – I think I actually penned in about February of 2000 as I had several months of sleepless nights, and then I revised it slightly in 2004.

She Stood There

In the midst of the shadows,
In a darkness that haunted,
She stood there still, silent, sorry, sad.

Plenty of time to think of days gone by;
Loves lost, loves gained; her sorrow remembered,
She stood there still, silent, sorry.

The seconds ticked to minutes,
The minutes onto hours,
She stood there still, silent.

She realized she could not have it all,
So she settled for less; but yet only the best,
She stood there still.

With her eyes wide open, her head held high,
With a decision in mind,
She stood there no more.

*"She Stood There" is the first poem I ever remember writing.
I was a teenager; I penned it just before I left my childhood home.*

Writer. Author. Poet. Artist.
Semi-retired award-winning television-producer.
Minister and Retreat Leader.

"Twinkle" Marie Manning is an interfaith minister who has been leading workshops, retreats and seminars in the secular and spiritual worlds for more than two decades. She began writing poetry as a teenager and uses it to this day to process and share life's experiences.

She has a sanctuary location in Northern Maine where she hosts collaborative, nature-based, spiritual, artistic & writing retreats.

Her published works include *The Women of Spirit Series;*
The Blessing & Reflection Book Series;
The *Mora Mulberry* Children's Book Series;
Intentional Visualization, and her seminal theology book,
Living Life as a Prayer which was published in 2020.

Among her favorite types of poetry to write are 20-line pantoums.

www.TwinklesPlace.org

Poetry by "Twinkle" Marie Manning

www.ingramcontent.com/pod-product-compliance
Lightning Source LLC
Chambersburg PA
CBHW010408130526
44592CB00051B/2678